# Mindless War 2.0

## Prism Truths Notes #1

by

**Paul E. Vallely - MG, US Army (Ret)**

**and**

**John D. Trudel**

# Preface

This book is an update to **Reality Prism: A Raven Thriller** and to **Mindless War**, released in the summer and fall of 2022, respectively. The focus of our books is to describe and explain the myriad attacks on our Western Culture in general and the United States as the critical target and last bastion of freedom. **Reality Prism** is a memoir, a predictive thriller, a recent history of events, a tour through 21$^{st}$ Century geopolitics, and an **Endgame**.

It overviews the ripping apart of our Constitutional Republic by a pack of enemies, traitors, and deep state officials (both parties) who now serve themselves, not those who elected them. The authors highlight the "Awakening of America," the Global Shadow Government, and how we must stand united.

**Prism** is now in production, and we have dug deep into the forces ripping America and the world apart. This has been in process for a long time. Truth, justice, and the American Way have mainly been replaced by darker things, slowly, incrementally, under the surface.

The preface to **Prism** is an epiphany by one of the authors, General Paul Vallely, based on his personal experiences in Egypt when he co-chaired two US delegations in 2014 and 2015. So it is that this note starts with **another** epiphany.

For centuries, America has been the shining city on the hill, the land of opportunity, a unique Republic with liberty and justice for all. A home created by people thoroughly imbued with the aspiration for truth and understanding. A free society under the rule of law, with strong institutions of faith and family, and with foundational principles of honor, fidelity, and patriotism. A place where all citizens had **God-Given Rights** to things like free speech, self-defense, fair trials, and due process.

These have been displaced by immorality in our entertainment, dishonesty of our media and elected officials, intensive censorship in social media and the public square, the suppression of dissent, and, yes, even public safety, secure borders, and honest elections. Along with this came the dumbing down of schools run by irresponsible educators who led students to reject traditional values and norms. American Patriots have now been deemed "the most dangerous terrorists," including soccer moms who protest at their local school boards.

After the stolen 2020 election, the Biden administration even set up an Orwellian Ministry of Truth ("paused" due to public outrage) and redirected our military and federal agencies from War Fighting to political correctness, gender issues, and targeting political opponents and involvement in unnecessary no-win wars. We are going bankrupt because of reckless spending on socialist programs that our children and future generations will be forced to pay for.

We are witnessing the planned destruction of American and Western civilization. Some call it "The Great Reset." The values that formed our foundation are being undermined and erased by greed and deception, by godless materialist ideologies. Writing *Prism* caused deep concerns and heightened awareness.

**My epiphany:** *We are not going to make it without God. Returning to the past and tradition is no longer an adequate response to the tyranny of the Left.*

We stand at the brink, staring into the abyss. By this time, it is evident that Leftist ideologies are displacing and erasing our civilized society. We witness an inability of civilization itself to provide a coherent and effective resistance to them.

This situation is like something out of *Star Wars*. The **Dark Side** of "The Force" is powerful and much to be feared. A New World Order of unaccountable ruling elites will replace our civilization. This utopian omelet requires the end of freedom and the destruction of the middle class. It has been underway for decades. It is not a "conspiracy theory," it is accurate. *Reality Prism* speaks to this. It offers solutions.

The radical Left is proficient in lies and deceit. That is what they do. Marxists, Communists, Socialists, Anarchists, et al. And, yes, now Democrats, Fake News, and most of the DC swamp. Naturally, those of the New World Order and The Great Reset do the same. Nazis were excellent at that, and at least one who served under Hitler, George Soros, is still alive. He has said publicly that those were the best days of his life. Others are, surprisingly, found in Ukraine. Not neo-Nazis, the old breed, the same as under Hitler.

Klaus Schwab, the head of the World Economic Forum, does have family roots going back to Hitler. His father, Eugen Schwab, was a close confidant of Hitler and ran a factory with forced laborers, including POWs. Proof that "Dad" was officially a Hitler Nazi is debated. Klaus was not. He was too young.

Incredibly, Klaus, who did not even live in the United States, was able to position himself with a front-row seat to the 9/11 World Trade Center attacks. On 11 September 2001, he sat having breakfast in the Park East Synagogue in New York City with Rabbi Arthur Schneier, across the street from the Towers. Klaus admits that one of his biggest influences was his college professor, Henry Kissinger.

So, is Klaus Schwab a kindly old uncle figure wishing to do good for humanity, or the son of a Nazi collaborator who used slave labor and aided Nazi efforts to obtain the first atomic bomb? I suppose that depends on who writes the history. Klaus does often have a front-row seat when tragedy approaches.

Saul Alinsky dedicated his book, **Rules for Radicals** to **Lucifer**. Hillary Clinton was a **fervent** Alinsky supporter. Obama **taught** Alinsky tactics.

BLM was founded by three Marxist organizers, who, yes, were Black and are now rich. Antifa, a worldwide organization, is modeled on Stalin's thugs. Try to hold a political rally or a peaceful protest, and they will be there to assault you and maybe to kill you.

Karl Marx said, **"The issue is not about the issue. The issue is about the Revolution."**

Thus, it is that we now live in a satanic time. This false reality, a life based on lies and deception, is ripping America apart. Some still see the old America. It is fading. Look harder. Sharpen your gaze. Take off your rose-colored glasses. Turn off your TV. Treason and Tyranny will create a new Dark Age if we allow it. A world of unaccountable ruling elites is the plan, and they have been working on the plan for decades.

Satanic evil is afoot. What we confront these days is not the traditional American reality. Not even close. It is the mirror image, the *Doppelgänger* of reality. Look hard. **The end of freedom.** Can you see it?

According to German folklore, all living creatures have an invisible spirit double identical to the living individual. These second selves are perceived as being distinct from ghosts (which appear only after death), and sometimes they are described as the spiritual opposite or negative of their human counterparts. German writers coined the word *Doppelgänger* (from *Doppel-*, meaning "double," and -*gänger*, meaning "goer") to refer to such specters of reality. The satanic side is becoming dominant.

Americans are already divided and denied our fundamental right to assemble. Schools and churches are closed, liquor stores are open, and drugs and crack pipes are free. Our borders are wide open, but we send weapons and money to the corrupt county to keep their borders safe. We risk an unnecessary war, a possible nuclear war, against a country that has not harmed us and does not threaten us.

Martin Luther King said he longed for a time when "All men (all of mankind) would be judged by their character, not by the color of their skin."

We almost made it, but Kennedy was killed, and Leftists like Lyndon Johnson knowingly turned the "Civil Rights Act" into "The Great Society." The radical Left made Blacks dependent on the government and thus trapped them in squalid, decaying, crime-ridden cities with failed schools run by drug gangs.

Blacks used to have strong religious and family ties. Welfare destroyed Black Families and Black Churches. It will be a long road back. There are several generations where no family has ever held a legal job. Exceptions like Ben Carson are rare, and that is a shame.

Trends like "Social Justice" exactly **reverse** the American Ethic. Rewards are based on gender, race, or compliance, not ability. We must have a Black Vagina on the Supreme Court….

As C. S. Lewis pointed out in *The Great Divorce*, good and evil cannot coexist. They are irreconcilable opposites, and the conflict between them is eternal. Evil must be fully understood and rejected. Evil can be undone, but it cannot develop into good. Time does not heal it.

Today we suffer not just Marxism and Socialism but neo-Marxism, Critical Theories, and more:

- Anti-colonialism
- Critical Race Theory
- Anti-racism
- White Patriarchy
- White Privilege
- White Fragility
- Toxic Masculinity
- Radical Feminism
- Queer Theory
- Gender Studies
- Intersectionality
- Political Correctness
- Social Justice

In the United States, these theories are now entrenched in society and government. Those who oppose them in the name of traditional values are branded as racist, homophobic, and fascistic. Major media outlets and social media now accept the dictates of this radical Leftist movement, suppressing speech, canceling alternative voices, and dehumanizing any who objects. **Families are being erased**.

Likewise, things like killing babies and selling their body parts for profit were unthinkable just a few years ago. Genocide by forced medication violates the Nuremberg Code, every article of which has been violated, all of which call for capital punishment. Lies to cover up such things are the new norm.

All that is evil, but funding all this with government money, selling the baby parts to unaccountable medical firms in return for generous donations to Democrats (and some Republicans), is legalized immoral money laundering on a massive scale. At this writing, the act of having the Supreme Court review this has spawned the same groups who **B**urn, **L**oot, and **M**urder in our cities to target the SCOTUS judges in their homes in violation of Federal Law. A crime that repeats and goes unpunished.

To allow such evil is to allow the completion of our national destruction. Shame on us. This is not acceptable. Killing babies for profit and political advantage surely justifies the use of words like **demonic** and **satanic**.

So does our waiting for God to fix it. He gave us free will, and **we** must be part of the solution. We cannot allow evil and wait for God to solve our problems. That is not how God designed our universe.

The only thing necessary for the Triumph of Good is for **Men and Women** to fulfill their God-given responsibilities. Divine providence is not dependent on God alone, but on humanity participating in the realization of the Creator's purpose. We have a role to play.

For what to do, I recommend four books, plus the Constitution:

- *The Triumph of Good*
- *People of the Lie*
- *American Marxism*
- *Reality Prism* (our book)

Resisting evil is about defeating human weakness. We are not going to make it without God. It is Cain vs. Able. All the theories listed above are profoundly anti-religious and anti-capitalist, feeding on Cain-type resentment, envy, victimhood, and murderous anger.

A friend (one more versed in biblical history than I am) says that God has three times given up, destroyed the world, and started over. **The Triumph of Good** is the most biblical of the recommended books. It has simple concepts, and one of its main points is that evil is built in from the time when God created the universe and that this is reported not just in the Christian Bible but in many other religions.

It gets back to God's hope for creation, about the disobedience of Lucifer, Adam, and Eve, and that the tale of Cain and Able is the revelation of truths and relationships that apply to this day. It argues that the Creator is restrained from removing evil from the world by the very nature and principles by which we humans were made. It claims that the family is the most important human institution and that children grow in understanding and love through the family.

The core argument is that the Cain-type ideology that (falsely, based on lies) claims to offer a utopian solution to all world problems is what plagues us now and that the actual outcomes of Leftist ideologies are tens of millions of deaths and decades of human suffering. The book asserts that Cain-type ideology has peaked in atheistic Marxism and Neo-Marxism.

This rings true to me. The above malignant theories are driven by envy, resentment, and a willingness to justify violence. Debates with those on the radical Left, in my experience, advocate resolving differences through accusations, interrogations, and violence, as if Cain were right all along.

The issue is not about the issue. Our troops in Vietnam were "Baby Killers." If you oppose someone of the Left, you will quickly be labeled as "racist," "domestic terrorist," "White supremacist," or something equally loathsome. You will be dehumanized. You may be "Borked" or worse.

The Democratic Party is the Party of Cain. The Great Reset will represent the triumph of Satan. The current situation justifies the use of the word "satanic." **The Dark Side is real.**

***

So, what did our Founding Fathers say?

*"We have no government armed with power capable of contending with human passions unbridled by morality and religion. Our Constitution was made only for moral and religious people. It is inadequate to the government of any other." – John Adams.*

John Adams made this statement in an October 13, 1789, address to the military.

*"And can the liberties of a nation be thought secure when we have removed their only firm basis, a conviction in the minds of the people that these liberties are of the gift of God? That they are not to be violated but with His wrath? Indeed, I*

tremble for my country when I reflect that God is just; that his justice cannot sleep forever." – Thomas Jefferson.

"While we are zealously performing the duties of good citizens and soldiers, we ought not to be inattentive to the higher duties of religion. To the distinguished character of Patriot, it should be our highest glory to add the more distinguished character of Christian." – George Washington.

\*\*\*

A few corners of social media still allow free speech. What do Americans active and paying attention today say? How do they see things? Here are samples from recent posts on Gab:

- Almost 80 percent of the country disapproves of Biden and the direction of our country. In any normal presidency, they would quickly change course and try to reverse the damage.
- The most concerning issue is that the Satanists (who are running the show) hate America and are determined to destroy it.
- They do not care if you approve of it or not.

\*\*\*

- They stigmatize the truth about gender by calling you a sexist.
- They stigmatize the truth about race by calling you a racist.

- They stigmatize the truth about homosexuals by calling them a homophobe.
- These are not arguments. They are stigmas to prevent you from telling the truth. This is why no one can have an honest, open conversation about these things without fear of repercussions.

\*\*\*

- "Whiteness" is the disease.
- Its course of treatment is dehumanization, hatred, and genocide.
- You are not cured until you cease to exist, but if you agree to cut your dick off and groom children, you'll be allowed visitation privileges.

\*\*\*

Public school is out of the question for our children because God designs our children to become like the teacher:

"...everyone, when he is fully trained, will be like his teacher." (Luke 6:40)

\*\*\*

So, that was my epiphany. What we are facing today is Satanism, evil raw and real. God gave us free will. We must be part of the solution. We cannot wait for God to solve our problems.

John D. Trudel

## What are Mind War and Mindless War?

**Mind War** is the use of sophisticated deception to deceive an enemy and to plant false images in his mind to allow advantage. It is a military tactic.

**Mindless War** is a phrase that we have coined to describe the methods and controls being used destructively by Globalists, the New World Order, China, the Radical Left, and others to replace the "old order" of countries, independent nation-states with a world of total control by independent, unaccountable elites. Groups like the World Economic Forum and the UN have been working on this for decades.

Yes, this is the "Great Reset." The goals are documented in UN Agenda 2030 and other such documents. That is the subject of our book, *Reality Prism*. The goal of **Mind War** is to instill **fear** in society! *"Fear is the Mind Killer."* It drives the loss of judgment. False reality can be used to cause insane, self-destructive behavior.

In the past, genocides and tyranny came from the force. As Mao demonstrated, "From the barrel of a gun." Or, as Hitler showed, from military conquest and death camps. **Mind War** is a much more effective tactic.

Recent events show its success in getting Americans to surrender our notions of exceptionalism and all men (and women) of being equal. Our God-Given Freedoms—from the right to assemble, free speech, fair trials, innocent until proven guilty, honest elections, freedom of worship, the rule of law, and, of course, at the end, the right to bear arms—are all slipping away.

Victor Davis Hanson summarized it as "Americans are now entering uncharted, revolutionary territory... The traditional bedrocks of the American system are dissolving." He further stated, "So as the public pushes back, expect at the ground level more doxing, cancel culture, de-platforming, ministries of disinformation, swarming the private homes of officials they target for bullying, and likely violent demonstrations in our streets this summer." He states, "The common denominator in all of this is ideology overruling empiricism, common sense, and pragmatism. Ruling elites would rather accept politically correct failures and be unpopular than to be politically incorrect, successful, and popular." – *The Epoch Times* May 18–24, 2022.

As Hanson warned, it is time to "Imagine the unimaginable." Americans are entering the uncharted, revolutionary territory. We may witness things this year that once would have seemed unimaginable.

https://www.theepochtimes.com/imagine-the-unimaginable_4462701.html

In the end, of course, force will be used. That has already been signaled in many ways—shaming, lawlessness, lockdowns, riots, looting, school shootings, food shortages, gas rationing, and, yes, even Gulags. The Biden administration uses the Patriot Act to target soccer moms at school board meetings and political opponents with MAGA hats.

A looming disaster lies ahead as the elitists face a potential disaster at the polls in November 2022. The Democrats will do everything possible to turn the election in their favor. There is a high assurance of voter fraud, that another pandemic may be launched, and/or a crisis disaster be declared to forego and delay the November elections. In Ukraine, globalists are already seizing assets and imprisoning political opponents.

A "spiritual awakening" of the American people is becoming a reality as we suffer out-of-control inflation, exorbitant energy prices, crime, draining the Treasury further in support of Ukraine, and an out-of-control border. Americans must decide whether to continue to ignore the decay of the Left's insane destructive policies or to reassert the rights so bestowed by the US Constitution and the Bill of Rights.

We have witnessed far too many of the WOKE Left and big government socialism promoting throughout the masses anti-social behavior, violence, ever-increasing criminality, and grave hostility toward the police, law, and order, and middle-class values.

When will the American people rise to toss out the politicians who have placed their country and lives at grave risk? What will happen when we do?

The plan now is to control the information of US citizens and punish those who contest the "**Obiden**" regime. It is a sign that the Democrats and their minions are moving to totalitarianism. It is part of a strategy to *"Change America Forever,"*—according to Obama.

What started as a **Mind War** against people has turned into a **mindless war** against the masses. Mindless actions are done without justification or concern for the consequences: synonyms for these actions are idiotic and brainless.

This eBook is written to describe the background for controlling information by the despots of globalists, elitists, technology elitists, and programmed Left-wing, liberal mindsets of Democratic political operatives. Some are calling this *American Marxism*. Others call it the **New World Order**.

## Mind Control in the 21$^{st}$ Century

Mind control is also known as manipulation, thought reform, brainwashing, mental control, coercive persuasion, coercive control, malignant use of group dynamics, and many others. The fact that so many names indicate a lack of agreement allows for confusion and distortion (especially by those using it covertly for their benefit!!). Let us agree that mind control comes under persuasion and influence—how to change people's beliefs and behaviors.

Some will argue that everything is manipulation. However, in saying this, important distinctions are lost. It is much more helpful to think of influence as a continuum. At one end, we have ethical and respectful influences that respect the individual and his or her rights. On the other end, we have destructive influences that strip the person of their identity, independence, and ability to think critically or logically. It is at this end that we find destructive cults and sects. These groups use deception and mind control tactics to take advantage of the weaknesses, as well as the strengths, of the members to satisfy the needs and desires of the cult leaders themselves.

## So, what is Mind Control?

It is best to think of it as a system of influences that significantly disrupts an individual at their very core, at the level of their identity (their values, beliefs, preferences, decisions, behaviors, and relationships), creating a new pseudo-identity or pseudo-personality. It can, of course, be used in beneficial ways, for example, with addicts, but here we are talking about situations that are inherently bad or unethical.

The psychologist Philip Zimbardo says that mind control is a "process by which individual or collective freedom of choice and action is compromised by agents or agencies that modify or distort perception, motivation, effect, cognition, and/or behavioral outcomes." He suggests that everyone is susceptible to such manipulation.

It is not some ancient mystery known to a select few. It is a combination of words and group pressures, packaged in such a way that it allows a manipulator to create dependency in his or her followers, making their decisions for them while allowing them to think that they are independent and free to decide. The person being controlled is not aware of the influence process nor of the changes occurring within themselves.

## Mind Control vs. Brainwashing vs. Indoctrination

Steve Hassan makes an interesting distinction between mind control and brainwashing. He says, "In brainwashing, the victim knows the enemy. For example, prisoners of war know that the person doing the brainwashing and/or torture is an enemy. Often, they understand that remaining alive depends on changing their belief system. They are coerced, often with physical force, into doing things they would not normally do. However, when the victim escapes from the influence of the enemy, the effects of brainwashing frequently disappear.

"Mind control is more subtle and sophisticated. Often the person doing the manipulations is considered a friend or a teacher, so the victim is not trying to defend themselves. He or she may be a 'willing' participant and believing that the manipulator has their best interests in mind, they often provide confidential information willingly, which is then used against them to continue the mind control.

"That makes mind control as dangerous, if not more so, than physical coercion. In other words, it can be even more effective than torture, physical abuse, or drugs. That is worth repeating. In mind control, there may be no physical coercion or violence, but it still can be much more effective in controlling a person. That is because coercion can change behavior, but coercive persuasion (mind control) will change beliefs, attitudes, thinking processes, and behavior (a personality change). And the 'victim' happily and actively participates in the changes, believing it is best for them!"

(Steven Alan Hassan is an American author, educator, Ph.D., and mental health counselor specializing in destructive cults. The media has described him as "one of the world's foremost experts on mind control, cults and similar destructive organizations," though social scientists are divided on his work. He is a former member of the Unification Church, founded Ex-Moon Inc. in 1979, and in 1999 founded the Freedom of Mind Resource Center. He has written on mind control and how to help people the experience has harmed.)

To accept that someone they trusted and liked has deceived and manipulated them is exceedingly difficult for people. This is one of the reasons that it is challenging for dupes to recognize mind control. Even when the victim is free of the influence of the manipulative personality, **the attitudes, beliefs, and behaviors persist**, in large part because the victim believes they have made these decisions themselves (the effects of decisions we make ourselves are stronger and more long-lasting than decisions we know we have been pushed to make), and, in part, because the person does not want to admit that they have been manipulated without their knowledge; they don't want to believe that a friend has tricked them.

## Who Uses Mind War?

We have evidence today that the US Military elite (The Generals and Admirals) force-fed the members of our Armed Forces as well as the cadets and midshipmen at our academies with Critical Race Theory and forced vaccinations.

Who else would use these techniques, destroying the lives of others for their selfish benefit? Or manipulating others simply because they can or because they want to control? The answer is psychopaths or sociopaths https://www.decision-making-confidence.com/sociopath-definition.html, and narcissists. Extremely manipulative men and women who use mind control to manipulate others are often narcissists.

They can do it so well because they have no conscience. These are "People of the lie." Such people tend to gravitate to places where they can wield power over others. They have always been with us. It is in the Bible. Such behavior is in the teachings of Marx and Alinsky.

Because people do not know exactly what a psychopath or a narcissist is, the manipulator is often called something else: an abusive wife or husband https://www.decision-making-confidence.com/controlling-husband.html,
a jealous boyfriend, a verbally abusive man, or a very strict boss. Closer examination often reveals that these people have personality disorders.

## Who is Susceptible to Mind War?

Every person is susceptible. That includes you! It is a myth that only weak and vulnerable people are susceptible or that there is something wrong with them. The belief that "it would never happen to me" makes a person particularly susceptible to mind control tools because they are not on the lookout for them!

## Game on! The Gloves Are Off

In April 2022, Barack Obama used his platform as a former US President to proclaim to "fight disinformation." In other words, to censor political speech damaging to the political elitists—America's ruling class. Lee Smith authored an outstanding article on controlling information in America, which was published in THE EPOCH TIMES and ran from May 4–10. Obama and his puppet, Joe Biden, intentionally promoted censorship to protect the Left-wing elitists.

Obviously, the goal is the move to a one-party system by marginalizing all other parties. Democrats in 2022 could not relate any good news from the first two years of Joe Biden's presidency and knew that some action had to be taken before the mid-term elections. How do we bury the unwelcome news from the public and gain some advantage (cheating, as well) and not face a total trouncing in the November elections?

As we got to know, Obama has been running the White House through his messenger, Susan Rice, sitting and office in the Executive Office Building next to the White House proper. Puppeteer to Puppet, Obama to Biden, and these are your orders for the day. So, Joe's itinerary is laid out and guided daily, including his sojourns to Delaware and other trips to show the puppet is alive (barely) and doing his executive jobs. How clever? And, of course, the American people will never figure the charade out. Also, we must remember: *"Never let a crisis go to waste!"*

Obama has always been a divisive person. He also has been destructive; a political figure wrought with deception and fraud across many fronts. The desire of the Leftist/communists (see Peter Schweizer's book, *"Red Handed"* – How American Elites Get Rich Helping China Win) is to control information at all levels in our society and, of course, to punish and destroy all those that oppose their constructs. This is certainly a clear and present danger to America.

In May 2022, the White House and Secretary Mayorkas announced a "Disinformation Governance Board (Ministry of Truth)." This initiative has been placed on hold.

The Department of Homeland Security announced the creation of the Board to coordinate the federal government's activities related to countering disinformation, with an immediate focus on illegal immigration to the United States and the Russia-Ukraine crisis. The board was to be led by Nina Jankowicz, a former disinformation fellow at the Wilson Center and adviser to the Ukrainian Foreign Ministry, who has a history of controversial and misleading statements.

The devising of disinformation has become a controversial and polarizing matter. Liberals say disinformation, meaning false information spread deliberately and covertly, is a threat to democracy. Conservatives, though, increasingly say that the threat of disinformation is wrongly used as a cover to censor them. "It can only be assumed that the sole purpose of this new Disinformation Governance Board will be to marshal the power of the federal government to censor conservative and dissenting speech. Homeland security should focus on securing the homeland and protecting Americans, not on trying to create the embryo of a Ministry of Truth," GOP Rep. Ken Buck of Colorado told the *Washington Examiner.* Republicans are also concerned about a February 2022 bulletin from the Department of Homeland Security saying the federal government plans to work with public and private sector partners, including Big Tech companies, to reduce the "proliferation of false or misleading narratives, which sow discord or undermine public trust in U.S. government institutions."

The GOP also worries about the federal government and the DHS being distracted from the border crisis. "The Biden administration is creating yet another distraction that will divert Department of Homeland Security resources away from our southern border," Republican Rep. Greg Steube of Florida told the **Washington Examiner.** "DHS somehow found enough resources to create a Climate Change Action Plan, Equity Task Force, and a Disinformation Governance Board. This is mismanagement of taxpayer dollars at best.

The American people want our southern border secured immediately," Steube said.

"I'm going to go out on a limb here and gently suggest that having a Disinformation Governance Board operating out of the Department of Homeland Security is not exactly a reassuring thought," said Shadi Hamid, a senior fellow of foreign policy at the Brookings Institution, a left-of-center think tank.

Yet, Glenn Gerstell, former general counsel for the National Security Agency and now a senior adviser at the Center for Strategic and International Studies, said that fears about the board are overblown.

Social media companies could welcome government intervention to limit their liability for censoring and controlling free speech.

## Politics of Personal Destruction

Nothing demonstrates how mean-spirited and vile the Left can be in advancing its anti-American agenda than the politics of personal destruction. The politics of personal destruction is a contemptible strategy for gaining and retaining political power by destroying the opposition—not defeating but destroying. The principal tactic of Leftists who practice the politics of personal destruction is *character assassination.* Character assassination involves using innuendo, smearing, false accusations, and outright lies to portray a political opponent as unworthy of the office sought and an individual of such low character as unfit for any office. The worst examples in the recent history of how the Left uses character assassination to attack political opponents are the confirmation hearings for Supreme Court Justices Clarence Thomas and Brett Kavanaugh.

Both distinguished jurists were vilified, smeared, disparaged, and denigrated on national television to sway the votes of the Senate Judiciary Committee and derail their confirmation to the Supreme Court. The Left had two goals in mind. First, they wanted to destroy these two Supreme Court candidates to avoid tilting the court to the Right. Second, they wanted to send a message to future conservatives who might be nominated to the bench; a message that made clear they would pay the price for accepting a presidential nomination.

The worst fear of Leftist ideologues is a Supreme Court willing to overturn the *sine qua non* of the Left: *Roe v. Wade*, the case "legalizing" abortion. There is no issue more important to the Left than protecting abortion. Fear of the views of Clarence Thomas and Brett Kavanaugh on abortion is why the Left tried hard to derail their confirmations to the Supreme Court. However, in the process, they overplayed their hands, revealing to the American people just how low the Left will go to advance its anti-American agenda and to hold on to gains it has made in this regard.

A lot of Americans were appalled and repulsed by the behavior of the Left in their attacks on Thomas and Kavanaugh, but what is even more disgusting than the Left's vile tactics is that so many Americans on the Left approved of them. Thomas and Kavanaugh survived the attacks of the Left and were confirmed, but the message to other conservatives who might be appointed in the future was sent loudly and clearly. One can only wonder what effect it has had.

It got worse when we had an unprecedented leak of confidential information from SCOTUS. More chilling is that the leaker, at this writing, has not been identified.

An even more despicable example of the politics of personal destruction can be found in the Left's attacks on Donald Trump. Having failed to prevent the confirmations of two conservative judges, the Left next turned its guns on the President of the United States, Donald Trump. Throughout his presidency and even before he took office, the Left unleashed an unrelenting smear campaign against him that continued even after he left office. He was falsely accused of colluding with the Russians to steal the election from Hillary Clinton. Then he was subjected to not just one but two partisan impeachments; one after he moved out of the

White House. Even out of office, Trump remained a favorite target of the Left.

The politics of personal destruction and character assassination demonstrate beyond any doubt just how low the Left will go to advance and protect its destructive agenda. This fact alone should be sufficient to convince Americans of the need to stand up to the Left, push back against its vile machinations, and reclaim our country for the sake of not just decency but survival.

## How Does Social Media Influence the Real World?

Social Media Marketing is one of the most potent forms of marketing available today. In recent years, the world has witnessed the blooming and ever-growing popularity of social media platforms. The power of social media cannot be ignored. The practical influence of social media on youth is noticeable, too. As technology is growing day by day, social media manages to bring and introduce new techniques, and it never fails to surprise us. Social media influences have a leading role to play in our lives.

When social media is appropriately used strategically, it not only helps in powerful marketing, but it is also one of the best forms of market research. Even though social media is powerful and unique, it is also true that a business cannot grow overnight into a success. It takes time and patience.

The art understands where you need to put your energy and how to work to get results.

Social media has not only influenced youths, but it has a profound influence on customers, too. It is a robust way to reach millions and billions of customers online. It not only helps you reach the national but international audience too.

We will discuss the powerful aspects of social media. Along with this, we will talk about the influence of social media on youth, customers, and businesses. We will discuss the benefits of social media, which makes it robust and impressive.

**Why social media?** Social media is a beautiful way to connect with people around the globe. Social media can provide real-time updates and information, and thus it has become the primary source of news for many. With functionalities that allow users to go live on social media platforms, it gives them the ability to share content with a vast audience coverage.

Why people share information, news, or anything else on social media is the real question here.

They share information to support a cause or when they strongly agree or disagree with an issue. When users share such posts, many of their followers re-share the same to create awareness about a particular issue.

Users on social media share valuable information on different topics to help others understand the same. For example, information and news on COVID-19, shared by the WHO, influence people, and make them more aware of the virus. But the influences extend in many other ways, like sharing information about products, services, or events.

Social media influences the relationships of a user with other people who thus use social media platforms to expand their circle and stay in touch with others. It is also an excellent place to acquire news and information.

People use social media to build their image, create an online presence, and interact with others to influence them.

## Social Media Influencers

People on social media platforms with a more significant following tend to share their opinions and news with their followers. These followers are in the count of millions. So, when people with millions of followers share their views, it significantly impacts them as they tend to trust the people they have been following. Undoubtedly, these people can influence the judgment or thought process of their followers. Therefore, they are also known as Social Media Influencers!

Social media platforms have become significant tools for influencers and companies. Influencers share their experiences with products they have been using, review newly launched products, and promote products. Based on their experiences, followers can decide whether to try a product.

On the other hand, companies can use these platforms to maintain transparency and show authenticity. These are different attempts to convince their followers to influence their decision-making. However, it is a two-way street. It means review systems on platforms like Facebook help people to evaluate the credibility of different companies or candidates. A user can review an online retail store, rate the food of a restaurant, the value of a book, or the appeal of a political candidate.

This process can be easily weaponized. Before blacklisting and banning were allowed, the primary weapon was using "trolls" (paid or false accounts) to bias viewer opinions. A more subtle and better weapon used by Big Tech was using biased search engines (like Google) to weaponize what users saw when they searched for a product or political candidate.

Social media amplifies **Mind War** to nuclear levels. A candidate can be demonized and blacklisted, as both Facebook and Twitter did to President Trump. Or boosted, as they did with an unseen Biden who "won" without campaigning.

Social media easily manipulates stock values. At the time of this writing, the multi-billion-dollar purchase of Twitter by Elon Musk faces legal action. Half the Twitter users may not be accurate. There are also "troll farms"—huge buildings with workstations holding multiple phones so one person can imitate many real customers. There are also "bots"—AI-based computer systems that fake human responses. By some accounts, half the alleged Twitter accounts may be "bots."

## Military PSYOPS

As a side note, let us examine how military psychological operations (both strategic and tactical) are conducted. Military Psychological Operations, abbreviated as PSYOP, are operations that aim to influence the feelings, motivations, and objective reasoning of audiences, as well as the behavior of governments, organizations, groups, and individuals. These operations involve the dissemination of selected information and indicators to audiences. In the United States, psychological operations are conducted with the goal of inducing or reinforcing behaviors that are thought to be beneficial to US interests. They play a significant role in the United States' ability to engage in a wide variety of operations across the fields of diplomacy, information, defense, and the economy. They are helpful in peace and war and may be employed in any situation.

It is strictly unlawful for members of the United States Psychological Operations (PSYOPS) personnel to make any effort, anywhere in the world, to sway the attitudes of "US individuals," which includes citizens and residents. During times of calamity or crisis, however, commanders may make use of PSYOP units in order to deliver public information to audiences in the United States. In accordance with the directive, it is the provision of information assistance to a noncombatant evacuation operation (NEO) by PSYOP personnel to convey evacuation information to nationals of the United States and third countries. During the rescue efforts in the aftermath of Hurricane Andrew in 1992, the use of PSYOP troops to disseminate vital public information to an audience in the United States was pioneered. Tactical Psychological Operations teams, also known as TPTs, were utilized so that information on the locations of relief shelters and facilities could be broadcast over loudspeakers.

During these types of Defense Support of Civil Authorities (DSCA) operations, military public affairs activities, military, civil authority information support (CAIS) activities, public information actions, and access for the news media to the DSCA operational area are all subject to approval by the federal department or agency that has been assigned primary responsibility for managing and coordinating a particular emergency support function.

Since October 2018, it has been possible for the Department of Homeland Security to instruct PSYOP soldiers to be deployed domestically for CAIS actions during times of emergency. In situations like these, Policy and Department of Defense instructions stipulate that PSYOP soldiers are only allowed to broadcast and disseminate publicly available material. During times of domestic emergency, PSYOP troops, when permitted to be used in this capacity, make use of their capabilities in the areas of media development, production, and distribution to send information to the general public as well as other vital information. Their sole purpose is to disseminate information.

## The Benefits of Using Non-Lethal Methods to Create an Atmosphere of Fear Through Mind War

Hermann Göring, the head of the Nazi Party, was quoted as saying that "The people do not desire war, but they can always be brought to the bidding of the leaders." Göring was referring to the fact that people may be induced to fear and support a conflict that they would otherwise reject. This is a simple task. All you must do is remind them they are under assault and criticize pacifists for their lack of patriotism and for putting the country in danger by not standing up for the nation. It operates in the same manner in every nation.

According to Zbigniew Brzezinski, who served as the former US National Security Advisor, the term "War on Terror" was explicitly chosen to incite a culture of fear on purpose because it "obscures reason, intensifies emotions, and makes it easier for demagogic politicians to mobilize the public on behalf of the policies they want to pursue."

According to Frank Furedi, a writer for *Spiked* magazine and a former professor of sociology, the culture of dread that exists today did not start with the destruction of the World Trade Center. Long before September 11, he claims, there was widespread public worry over a variety of issues, including but not limited to genetically modified crops, mobile phones, global warming, and foot-and-mouth disease.

## Impact of the Media

The consumption of mass media has had a profound effect on instilling the fear of terrorism in the United States, though acts of terror are a rare phenomenon.[1] Beginning in the 1960s, George Gerbner and his colleagues have accelerated the study of the relationship between media consumption and the fear of crime. According to Gerbner, television and other forms of mass media create a worldview that is reflective of "recurrent media messages" rather than one that is based on reality. [1] Many Americans are exposed to some form of media daily, with television and social media platforms being the most used methods to receive both local and international news. As such, this is how most receive news and details that center around violent crime and acts of terror. With the rise in the use of smartphones and social media, people are bombarded with constant news updates and can read stories related to terrorism and stories from all corners of the globe. Media fuels fear of terrorism and other threats to national security, which have adverse psychological effects on the population, such as depression, anxiety, and insomnia. Politicians conduct interviews, televised or otherwise, and utilize their social media platforms immediately after violent crimes and terrorist acts, to further cement the fear of terrorism into the minds of their constituents.

It was seventy-five years ago, on Jan. 6, 1941, that President Franklin Roosevelt stood to deliver the State of the Union address that would become one of his most famous. "At no previous time has American security been as seriously threatened from without as it is today," Roosevelt admitted, but he still had hope for a future that would encompass the "four essential human freedoms"—including freedom from fear. And when Pearl Harbor was attacked at the end of that year, news reports from the time showed that Americans indeed responded with determination more than fear.

Three-quarters of a century later, a poll released in December found that Americans are more fearful of terrorism than at any point since Sept. 11, 2001. And while recent events like the attacks in ISIS-inspired attacks in Paris and the fatal shootings in San Bernardino, California, may have Americans particularly on edge, experts say that Roosevelt's advice has gone unheeded for some time.

"My research starts in the 1980s and goes more or less till now, and there have been very high fear levels in the U.S. continuously," says Barry Glassner, President of Lewis and Clark Community College and author of *The Culture of Fear*: *Why Americans Are Afraid of the Wrong Things*.

One substantial change over the last half-century has been the proliferation of a politics of fear. Stearns identifies Lyndon Johnson's 1964 "Daisy" Function as the first fear-based political ad and says that fear's presence in American discourse has only increased since then. Glassner agrees that politicians, companies, and the media have played a big part in the change, figuring out how to trigger fear and using that knowledge more frequently. Technology is part of it, too, though something like the Lindberg baby news of the child's disappearance today would appear round-the-clock on cable, social media, or via AMBER Alerts to Americans' phones.

## Truth, Honesty, and Virtue can Defeat Mind War

There is little controversy that honesty is a virtue. It is an excellence of character. It promotes trust, fosters healthy relationships, strengthens organizations and societies, and prevents harm.

Sadly, though, honesty has gone missing in recent decades. It is absent from academic research. It is rare in society. And it is not commonly found in discussions of how to become a better person. People, including elected officials, lie under oath in testimony to Congress without consequences.

A suggestion is to have regular moral reminders of honesty in our lives. Such reminders can make our moral norms salient, such that they more actively work against a desire to cheat, lie, or steal. Honesty reminders can take a wide variety of forms, including diaries, readings, signs, and emails. There can also be institutional reminders that we encounter at work or school.

One such moral reminder in many schools is an honor code, which students must sign before taking a test.

A final suggestion is to work against our desire to cheat, a desire that can be especially powerful when we think we can get away with cheating and benefit in the process. Such a desire is at work in studies such as those by Shu and Bryan, mentioned earlier, and introspectively, we can all recognize moments in our lives when it has influenced us as well.

One straightforward way to try to rein it is to increase the policing of cheating and impose harsher penalties on those found guilty. For instance, with the move in education toward take-home exams during the COVID-19 pandemic, computer surveillance of students taking those exams has become a big business, although not without giving rise to several moral and psychological concerns.

Increased policing and punishment for cheating might be effective in curbing dishonest behavior, although that, too, is an empirical claim that needs further study. But, even if it does, that is not enough to foster the virtue of honesty. As I said earlier, motivation matters too. Here, the motivation for not cheating would be punishment avoidance, which is purely self-interested. While I tried to be very generous about what can count as honest motivation, this one is not going to make it on the list.

Instead, the desire to cheat could be diminished in a more virtuous manner by fostering other virtues alongside honesty, such as friendship and love. If someone is genuinely my friend, I want what is best for that person, even if it is at the expense of my self-interest. Similarly, if I love others and care deeply for them, I am concerned about their good. The deeper the friendship and love, the less likely we would be dishonest with others for our gain.

## The Awakening

Awakening is starting to understand something, usually something significant, that leads to a new and better understanding of events. In 1776, Americans awoke to the fact that to stay free and prosper, they must separate their fortunes from England. In the 21st century, America slept as Marxism (disguised as Progressive Socialism) relentlessly crept into our society. Globalism, the rise of unaccountable ruling elites, and an ascendant Communist China were dismantling our great country not by direct warfare but from within.

It was like a beautiful building being destroyed by destructive waves of termites. There was no Pearl Harbor, no major issue that divided us like the Civil War, and no significant foreign war or power that openly threatened us militarily. China's **Three Warfares** doctrine underpins the Chinese Communist Party's (CCP) plan to instead conquer the free world without firing a shot. [So far, it is working.]

From the time our Constitution was framed, Americans argued intensely but honestly. It was one of our strengths. Quite often, widely differing groups would come to better solutions than had advocated. [No, it did not always work. There was a Civil War that almost destroyed us.]

We were multiethnic but of a common culture. Our own unique culture. The motto **E Pluribus Unum**, "One out of Many," first proposed by the First Continental Congress in 1782, summed it up perfectly.

There were countless benefits: equality under the law, freedom of religion, strong families, a striving for exceptionalism, freedom, and the pursuit of happiness. We were safe. We were prosperous. Life was good. We were living "The American Dream," and the entire world knew it.

Unfortunately, we had powerful enemies who knew our strengths and weaknesses. Mostly forgotten now is the Cold War (1945–1990), a time when two generations lived in fear, a time of fallout shelters, hoarding food, and ***Doctor Strangelove***.

Some military leaders (e.g., Patton and MacArthur), seeing Communism as the enemy and deeming America more powerful, wanted to end the threat. That was something that America's public and political leadership would not accept. Neither side wanted to start a war that might go nuclear. Geopolitical policy became MAD—Mutually Assured Destruction. It sounded mad indeed, but it worked for a time.

It worked only because we had seasoned leadership and a bipolar world. Both sides knew the Russians would never risk their steady gains by overstepping. Proxy wars were tolerated, but both sides worked to avoid direct confrontation and restrain allies. With a few exceptions (e.g., USS Pueblo, U2) both kept an unwritten agreement to not kill spies or interfere with mutual surveillance.

During the Korean War, especially after China escalated, both sides pretended the UN could prevent or end conflicts. It never has, of course, so, after Cuba, a Red Telephone hotline was added between the White House and the Kremlin to avoid mistakes.

Eisenhower was a seasoned, trusted wartime leader, but even he warned us strongly of a dangerous "Military Industrial Complex." People around the world were terrified. What would happen when ambitious, inexperienced politicians inevitably took over? One mistake could turn the world into a cinder.

Along came John Kennedy, who wanted "softer" options. His policy was "Measured Response." If Communists attacked, we would respond with the same force and hold the stalemate. The Russians, expert chess players, liked that. So did China. Hence, Vietnam—a land war in Asia.

Kennedy was backing away from that policy before he was assassinated, but the die was cast. No more "Cold War," but a period of "pretend peace," constant limited war, insurgency, and bloodshed. (Eisenhower warned us of this in his farewell address. His warning has proved to be prophetic.)

In America, we suffered violent Leftist-incited rioting, burning, and spitting on our soldiers sent to fight America's far-off enemies. Bill Ayers, a mentor to Obama, bombed the

Pentagon and later bragged about it. John Kerry, as a serving Navy Reserve officer, met with the North Vietnamese in Paris during the Vietnam "Peace Talks." Neither was ever held accountable.

Secretary of Defense McNamara, an accountant, kept a tally of body counts on the nightly news to prove we were winning. Communists could not care less. Life was cheap. The Tet Offensive was a military disaster for North Vietnam (massive casualties and no regional capitols were held). Still, thanks to Walter Cronkite (then highly trusted), who told the public we had lost badly, it was a significant media victory for the Left.

Three years after the peace treaty was signed, ending the war, Democrats (including Biden) in Congress cut off military aid. America abandoned South Vietnam, the embassy fell, and "the Killing Fields" followed.

Much later, Reagan ended the Cold War, the Berlin Wall came down, and we won. The USSR dissolved. As one intel official put it, the military mission shifted from slaying dragons, something we had mastered, to killing nests of snakes, foreign and domestic. A new threat. One that is close and deadly.

And so it is that our enemies, foreign and domestic, now work to destroy America by exploiting our freedom and tolerance by dividing us into polarized groups. They have worked at this not for years, but for decades. Even China, now our greatest foreign threat, meticulously avoids nuclear threats. It is winning by a mix of biowarfare and 4th Generation Mind War, with the bioweapons funded by US taxpayers.

When the masks went on for COVID, they came off for the planned destruction of America. Now, after a stolen election, we get to choose between Freedom and Tyranny. Some in power, including Democrats, Fake News, Big Tech, Big Pharma, the Washington Swamp, unaccountable bureaucracies, the FBI, and the CIA may prefer Tyranny. *Total control may keep them in power.*

Minor changes can have a massive impact. Most think the Department of Education has been around forever. No. The story of DOE started in 1867 under Andrew Johnson, but only to collect statistics on education. These were excellent until 1979, when Jimmy Carter made a federal takeover of education. The Department of Education is now in a cabinet position, and our schools are failing. Carter also set up the SES, the "Senior Executive Service," which now prevents the majority of Swamp Bureaucrats from being fired.

Since then, K-12 education has slipped to where one can no longer find credible US government data. According to a *Business Insider* report in 2018, the United States ranked 38th in math scores and 24th in science, falling from top excellence to not even being in the top twenty. Some states (e.g., Oregon) no longer require proficiency in math, reading, or science for High School graduation.

Homeschooling and charter schools, fiercely resisted by bureaucrats and teachers' unions, are in demand. Black people trapped in the inner cities are desperate for better schools and more law enforcement, but are getting the reverse.

Worse yet is that schools, including universities, have shifted from teaching "how to learn" to "what to learn," which includes indoctrination about "Critical Race Theory" and revisionist history, like "The 1619 Project."

Parents who dare to object at school board meetings are now threatened with being targeted by the FBI as **terrorists** under the Patriot Act. Marxists, well-funded and now in power, say children belong to the State [Hillary's "It takes a village to raise a child."]. Parents are enraged.

Free speech is banned on college campuses. That is now spreading to all schools and other venues. Who dares walk through a large city wearing a MAGA hat? It is deemed a "hate crime."

Beyond that, the DC bureaucracies have grown exponentially and are now entirely unaccountable. They develop more pages of rules every year than Congress. You cannot fire them, and the rules they pass have the power of law. **Biden's**

**damaging "Vaccine Mandate" was justified by a press release!**

You can go to prison for breaking some "law" never passed by any elected, accountable official. In cases like Biden's "Vaccine Mandate" (which does not even exist), a press release was deemed sufficient to justify mass firings and even an odd speech by Biden himself that demonized healthy, law-abiding Americans (including healthcare workers and the military) who declined to take problematic experimental vaccines. He even accused them of destroying the healthcare system and selfishly taking up hospital space.

Such a situation would have been unimaginable to America's founders. There are many other examples.

The Democratic Party (and key Republicans) decided to move swiftly to the Left long before the 2020 election brought about the ousting of their brutal enemy, Donald J. Trump, and the election of Joe Biden as America's new leader.

The People's Republic of China (PRC) made a declaration of a People's War against the USA in retaliation for Trump's policies that embarrassed the PRC and revealed their dishonest trade policy. The declaration was followed by biological warfare attacks employing the COVID-19 virus. PSYOPS and cyber-warfare accompanied these aggressive operations to steal the 2020 elections. The CCP bribed the

Biden family, making the POTUS an agent of the CCP. Biden and others then collaborated with Communist China to harness American policy and operations to PRC interests, which explains the disastrous American withdrawal from Afghanistan.

We have learned from email traffic released by whistleblowers that the Democrats collaborated with the CCP to develop the Wuhan virus, or COVID-19. It is the same virus that has been used by the CCP to wage biological warfare against the USA. The attacks have inflicted great harm and constitute a genocidal war crime that has morphed into a worldwide pandemic.

Evidence obtained by Project Veritas exposed the Biden administration's use of the COVID pandemic for domestic political purposes, which has since been admitted publicly. The messages below reveal evidence of the use of the COVID virus to advance the domestic policy of the Democrats.

There is hard evidence that has exposed the conspiracy to use the pandemic for political purposes. Connecting the dots with the Project Veritas evidence, we see the logic that drives the Biden COVID-19 narrative.

The rise of the West was based on four primary victories of reason. The first was the development of faith in progress within Christian theology. The second victory was the way that faith in progress translated into technical and organizational innovations, many of them fostered by monastic estates. The third was that thanks to Christian theology, reason informed political philosophy and practice to the extent that responsive states, sustaining a substantial degree of personal freedom, appeared in medieval Europe. The final victory involved the application of reason to commerce, resulting in the development of capitalism within the safe havens provided by responsive states. These were the victories by which the West won.

Communist advocacy presumes simultaneous attacks on the political, military, arts, judicial, science, education, and religious components of society. By seeding crazy ideas into policies across the board—the Left creates a Potemkin Village sense of unreality. Specifically, if leaders can create a unified impression of maniacal decision-making, the elites can foster a miasma of doom and powerlessness in the face of bizarre standards. The Democrats must either destroy a society or project out that the society is undermined and, therefore, insolvent. Then, a socialist imperative will be imposed.

For the Democrats to purposely build a national program from contradictions and lies while pretending their actions are above criticism is certifiable madness. Leftism demands its followers sacrifice honesty in the battle for world socialism. Specifically, Biden's pathological lying is typical of several mental health disorders, or it might be confabulation as the result of lost cognition. Or, according to Christian tradition, lying is the hallmark of Satan, indicating deep spiritual sickness.

Indeed, Marxism's radioactive cynicism presupposes lying as a hallowed tactic. One can describe criminal insanity as living in a perpetual state of dishonesty. In all events, perpetual dissembling cannot be sustained unless the entire populace becomes debased, cynical, and inured to deceit. As this transition is occurring in America, we are simultaneously devolving toward another third-world failure. Please pray for the USA.

America is filled with a lot of lazy thinkers who would instead let somebody else do the job for them. They do not know what they believe because they do not know who they are. All they care about is holding a popular opinion. Thinking frightens them because they do not know where it will lead them; they might even wander off the thought reservation and be ridiculed by others.

Many culprits can be blamed for this, but in the end, we are each responsible for what we believe, regardless of how we got there. If we believe a liar, especially for the accolades of men, we will, in the end, pay the price. God alone is the only one who will not lie to us, but do we listen to Him? He frequently asks in His Word: "Am I a man that I should lie?"

The devil will do his best to lie to us because it is a way of stealing the good that God has planned for us. The devil only has the power that we give him if we believe his lies. Come to think of it, the same is true of evil people: they will continue to lie to us, but we only give them power over us when we believe their lies.

If you do not want to be ruled by the devil and his liars, stop believing them. Even easier, stop listening to them or watching their media. Demand their evidence or search out your own. It's highly likely they have none. Their talking points are furnished by those who own them, but the evidence is more challenging to manufacture.

*That is why America has a court system, not a Ministry of Truth.*

## Welcome to 2023 and Mind War 2.0

So much has happened, much of it unprecedented in all of America's history. We have had hundreds of innocent citizens locked in Gulags (held without charges or legal counsel, and under harsh conditions, for almost two years) for a peaceful protest on January 6, 2021.

There was one death—the **only** one—of an unarmed female veteran (**Ashlie Babbitt**) who was shot down without warning by Capitol Police officer **Lt. Michael Byrd** who had a record of carelessness prior to this murder, firearms violations that should have justified his firing. Videos from that day show Byrd waving his gun around with his finger on the trigger, thus violating ordinary firearms safety procedures, and giving a signal that he'd already decided to shoot someone and was just trying to decide who.

Ashlie's murder has never seen a full investigation. But two years later, when her aged mother came for a peaceful protest to honor her dead daughter, she was arrested (for "jaywalking," with no traffic and in a zone flooded with the police!) and thrown into jail.

It gets stranger. The January 6 protests by unarmed citizens have been termed "an insurrection." How did that happen, and who was responsible? According to Kevin McCarthy (now House Majority leader) and a DOD IG report, it was General Milley, the same person who had said he'd warn the Chinese of any planned actions by President Trump (treason), and the man responsible for the Afghanistan debacle that left dead Americans and a trove of brand-new American weapons for the Taliban.

This is important to note. From the DOD IG report on January 6, DOJ was responsible, but, in reality, Milley ran the show. Why this charade? Two reasons seem likely. First off, only an "insurrection" gives the military any possible grounds to use armed force against unarmed civilians, and also, leading an insurrection (e.g., like the Civil War) would potentially ban President Trump from protesting the most likely stolen election of 2020.

DOD ran the show, but DOJ did the dirty work. Later the FBI piled on, with an unprecedented raid on President Trump's home. There was **extensive** evidence of election fraud (e.g., Zucker bucks, Zucker boxes, mishandled ballots, etc.) for the 2020 election, but **Mind War** prevailed. The evidence was never heard.

Instead, there were extensive hearings (unsuccessful) to charge President Trump with something. "Election Deniers" who dared to question the election were deemed "Domestic Terrorists." Joe Biden won from his basement without campaigning, and he even gave a speech about that, posed against a red background, like Stalin or Hitler.

More outrageous in some ways, the same happened in the 2022 election. Arizona took another hit. A popular candidate for governor faced an opponent who didn't even bother to campaign but was in charge of **running** the election. Arizona is still undergoing legal challenges. Election Fraud may have left Republicans (and America) with an open border, plus a lost governorship, and possibly also a lost Senate seat.

In any case, this tale of decline and disaster will see many books and movies and more Fake News. Already, the Biden Administration is in the news for the same crimes alleged to be committed by Trump. That is Alinsky 101, "Accuse them of what you do yourself."

We will leave all that to others. This small book is focused on *Mind War*, but we needed to give context.

The general background is available to any who are paying attention. A border controlled by violent cartels, soaring crime rates, at least 11 to 22 million illegals here (**source:** MIT Yale 2018, more now), homelessness, more young Americans dying from fentanyl each year than did during the entire Vietnam war, parents being arrested for protesting at school boards, children being groomed, failed schools, shortages, inflation, and a plague of COVID and deaths from jabs, including children, pilots, and professional athletes in their prime.

Klaus Schwab, Founder and Chairman of the **World Economic Forum** says in his book *Covid-19: The Great Reset* that he wants to eliminate at least <u>**four billion**</u> "useless eaters" by the year 2050 by means of limited wars, organized epidemics, and starvation. The details for those who survive are even more horrific.

We suggest it is past time to look hard through a *Reality Prism* and be aware of **Mind War**.

## Testing examples of Successful Mind War

Some fortunate things have happened. We are now aware of the extreme censorship and de-platforming we have suffered in America. Elon Musk did us a huge favor when he purchased Twitter and started revealing Orwellian details.

We now know those in charge of censorship were government security people. The teams in control were the FBI, CIA, etc. We picked topics of significant events likely to be heavily censored. We did not test on the "woke" social media. Facebook is pure propaganda, and Twitter is just now coming back.

We looked to the places that were <u>not</u> being minded by the Government (e.g., Gab, etc.). That will give a pretty heavy "awareness" bias since many there fled or were banned. Plans are to repeat these tests on Twitter, assuming it survives and repopulates with a good cross-section of America.

On December 29, 2012,
President Barack Obama
signed HR 4310,
**The 2013 National Defense
Authorization Act.**

Section 1078 of the bill authorizes the use
of **propaganda** inside the US, which had
previously been banned since 1948 when
the Smith-Mundt Act was passed.

Here are the sample statements that we evaluated. We explored seven world-changing events, each with extensive "Fake News" reports and controversies that grabbed attention and rolled on for years.

1. A "lone gunman killed Kennedy."
2. John Brennan did NOT enable the 911 jihadists.
3. Benghazi was about a video.
4. There was no election fraud in 2020 or 2022.
5. George Floyd was killed by police, not by a massive drug OD.
6. Almost a hundred close Clinton associates DID die by suicide.
7. The Obama birth certificate was real.

In the context of our book, *Reality Prism*, could **Mind War** move perceptions from the **Reality Prism** to the **Political Prism** viewpoint? Would most "normies" (e.g., average Americans, focused on families, sports, and enjoying life) accept these distant, world-changing assertions as **accurate**?

Most did **not** deem the above statements as truthful. There were two "minority vote" clusters of exceptions. The outliers concerned 911 (now a distant memory) and George Floyd (the "Social Panic" that spawned riots, burned cities, made a fortune for Black Lives Matter, and resulted in defunding and demonizing the police).

Exposing those results, we did another survey. This one is on Substack, a bastion of free speech on social media. We asked if **Mind War** was effective. This audience thought it was and feared that it was.

**Did Mind War work? Did those "false reality" statements work?**

**60%** — "Yes, most of them did."

**20%** — "We must (again) outlaw Propaganda as NEWS!"

**20%** — "These lies tore America Apart."

**0%** — "No, this was not a problem."

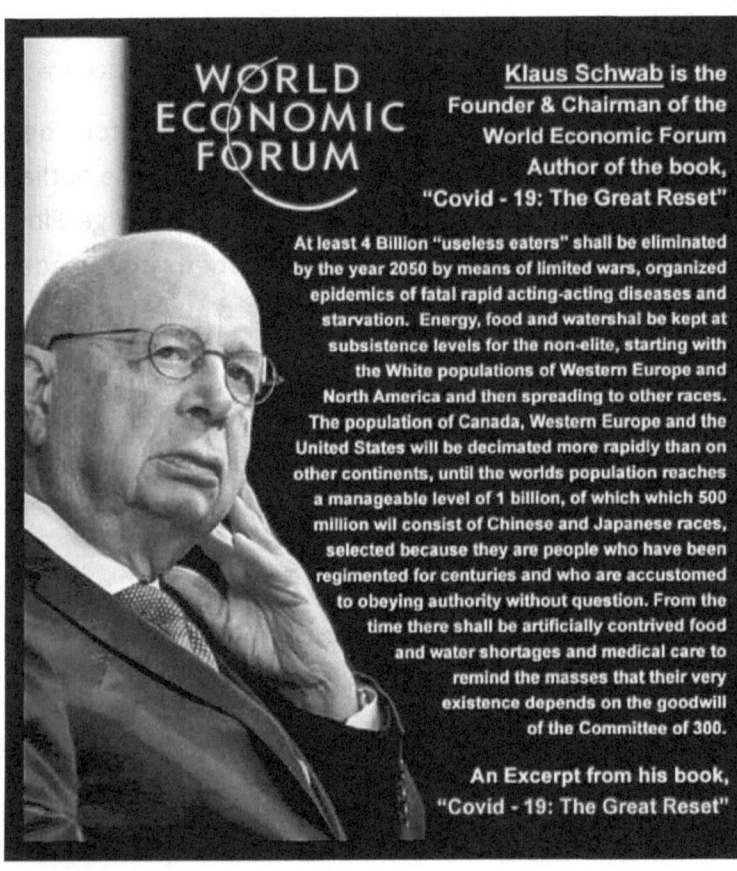

**WORLD ECONOMIC FORUM**

Klaus Schwab is the Founder & Chairman of the World Economic Forum Author of the book, "Covid - 19: The Great Reset"

At least 4 Billion "useless eaters" shall be eliminated by the year 2050 by means of limited wars, organized epidemics of fatal rapid acting-acting diseases and starvation. Energy, food and watershal be kept at subsistence levels for the non-elite, starting with the White populations of Western Europe and North America and then spreading to other races. The population of Canada, Western Europe and the United States will be decimated more rapidly than on other continents, until the worlds population reaches a manageable level of 1 billion, of which which 500 million wil consist of Chinese and Japanese races, selected because they are people who have been regimented for centuries and who are accustomed to obeying authority without question. From the time there shall be artificially contrived food and water shortages and medical care to remind the masses that their very existence depends on the goodwill of the Committee of 300.

An Excerpt from his book, "Covid - 19: The Great Reset"

For follow up, we asked about the purpose. It was **The Great Reset.**

The **New World Order**. Nation states replaced by unaccountable oligarchs.

Our sample group was aware and concerned. The end game is mass murder, constant war (e.g., Ukraine), and total control. For now, **Mind War** keeps many ignorant.

The end goal is FOCUSED GENOCIDE. Some races are to be erased totally, billions killed, and half of the survivors Japanese or Chinese, *"Because they are used to being controlled."*

WEF is like a bad James Bond movie. We are seeing the Kalergi Plan. It is real, and it is here.

## THE KALERGI PLAN: A Short History Lesson.

**Richard von Kalergi**
Founded the **EU** and wrote the Kalergi Plan, which aims to make unique races and cultures **extinct**.
**Visit:** bit.ly/2PiEPHh - **Google:** Kalergi Plan

**Warburgs, Baruchs, Rothschilds**
Are some of the **banking cartels** responsible for funding Kalergi's **genocidal ideology**.
**Visit:** bit.ly/2zG4nZl - **Google:** Rothschild Banking History

**The UN and the EU**
Execute the Plan, calling it **"Replacement Migration."** The UN **Migration Pact** also criminalizes criticism of immigration as "hate speech" (thought crime).
**Visit:** bit.ly/2rsuRJX & bit.ly/2UhjktM - **Google:** United States of Europe

**You?**
Eventually, this Plan will target every nation on Earth. Like, **save**, and **share** this image to spread awareness far and wide. Time to **stand against tyranny**.
**Visit:** bit.ly/2SnBisQ & bit.ly/2KXPAyc

**Elon Musk:**

*"WEF is increasingly becoming an unelected World Government that the people never asked for and don't want."*

WEF 2023 is full Fascist. Hard core tyranny. The masks are off, people are catching on, and they want to collapse America before Election 2024. A priority is to ban "hate speech" (= FREE SPEECH) this year!

FBI Director Wray gave a speech at WEF that the future was collaboration between the Big Tech and Government. This is how Mussolini defined Fascism. It is also treason.

**What is as powerful and more dangerous than Mind War?**

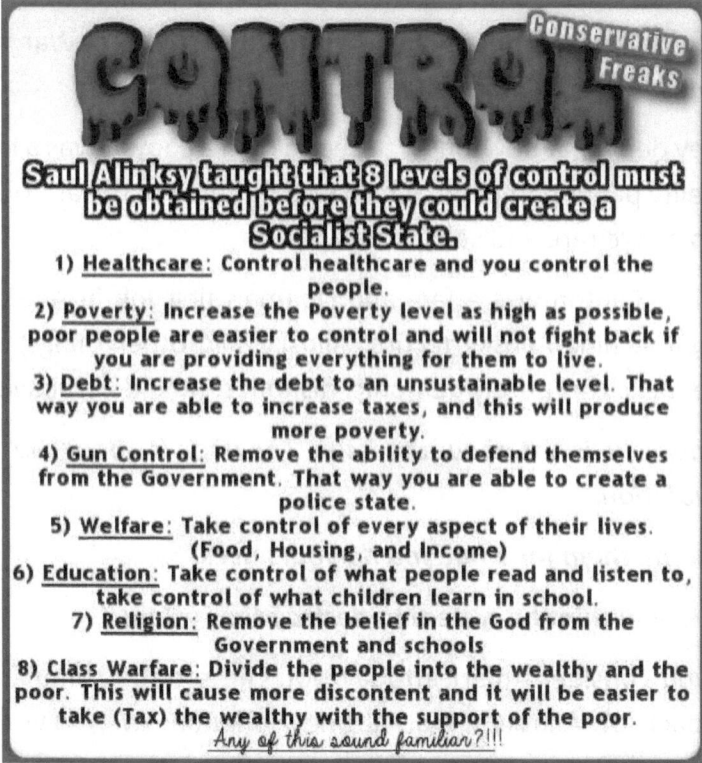

CONTROL

Conservative Freaks

Saul Alinsky taught that 8 levels of control must be obtained before they could create a Socialist State.

1) <u>Healthcare</u>: Control healthcare and you control the people.

2) <u>Poverty</u>: Increase the Poverty level as high as possible, poor people are easier to control and will not fight back if you are providing everything for them to live.

3) <u>Debt</u>: Increase the debt to an unsustainable level. That way you are able to increase taxes, and this will produce more poverty.

4) <u>Gun Control</u>: Remove the ability to defend themselves from the Government. That way you are able to create a police state.

5) <u>Welfare</u>: Take control of every aspect of their lives. (Food, Housing, and Income)

6) <u>Education</u>: Take control of what people read and listen to, take control of what children learn in school.

7) <u>Religion</u>: Remove the belief in the God from the Government and schools

8) <u>Class Warfare</u>: Divide the people into the wealthy and the poor. This will cause more discontent and it will be easier to take (Tax) the wealthy with the support of the poor.

*Any of this sound familiar?!!!*

The seven points surveyed were selected as **Mind War** examples, not just because they were key issues that hugely impacted America, but because they also showed how **Saul Alinsky's** tactics have been used to destroy American culture, norms, and values. Each of those disasters was to be amplified and exploited to have an increasing impact as time passed.

Before **Mind War** there was **Alinsky**. His book, *Rules for Radicals*, First Edition, came out in the early seventies, just before Alinsky's death in 1972 when the Vietnam War was raging. **The first edition was dedicated to Lucifer.**

They deny that now, but we used to own a copy. It was a low-quality paper pamphlet, which sold for about a dollar. Today, copies are rare and sell for over $100.

Hillary Clinton was a fan, and Obama's first job in America was teaching Alinsky tactics. Alinsky said other things, but the focus was purely demonic, dishonest, and destructive.

*"The issue is not about the issue. The issue is about the revolution."*

*"Blame them for what you do yourselves."*

*"Work within the system to destroy the system."*

If you consider America today, you can see the cumulative impact of Alinsky's evil. Crime, inflation, war, division, tyranny. We are on the way to being a Third World nation, on a roller coaster to Hell.

Note we say, "cumulative evil." Take event #2 we sampled, 9/11. There were 2,997 deaths, but at least 25,000 more died later. Not counting more from needless wars, etc. Call that the direct impact.

But look at other consequences. We set up a huge bureaucracy, TSA, which never caught a terrorist, but did control, intimidate, and harass millions of innocent Americans. We were indoctrinated into accepting scans, strip searches, and submission. We passed the Patriot Act to strip patriotic citizens of their rights. For the first time in history, we shut down our air traffic infrastructure. Now it can be shut down at will.

Now, decades later, we are seeing the completion of the destruction of our excellent air traffic system, except, so far, for the ruling elites with government transport or private jets. The kill shot was COVID, a bioweapon, followed by the "clot shots." Air travel became slow, unpleasant, unreliable, and expensive.

Wearing masks was always about control, but it was madness on airlines. Pilots, who always had good health and medical exams as a part of licensing, were forced to get vaccines of dubious value. The jabs were worse. Airline pilots were failing their EKG tests and, like some healthy young athletes, suffering heart failure. One captain died just after takeoff. His copilot saved the flight.

The final blow was if pilots refused to take the jabs, they were fired, and their careers were over. (The same for first responders, military, nurses, etc.) It was about control. It was a fraud. And now the ruling elites (of Devos and elsewhere) are deciding that THEY will only use pure-blood pilots. As during the lockdowns, with Nancy Pelosi and others, the rules and laws don't apply to them.

Here is the difference between **Alinsky's tactics** and **Mind War**. Both have power, but Mind War can be used for good.

Alinsky is pure evil. The policies we are seeing from Woke elites are all about control, destruction, and devastation, a path to a **New World Order** of rulers and serfs, masters, and slaves.

Those who oppose tyranny are no longer deemed to be patriots. Political opponents are dehumanized and threatened. Patriots shifted from baby killers to deplorable birthers, racists, election deniers, or domestic terrorists. Statues are toppled, history is erased, crime soars, and no one is safe.

What can reverse that? Perhaps Revolution and Civil War. Justice. Traitors being hanged. A Nuremberg 2.0. It may come to that. Or it may just come to national collapse and the New World Order.

Or it may be possible that outraged Americans, new leadership, and better tactics, including **Mind War**, could save us. Consider issue #7, the Obama Birth certificate issue.

Endless debate and litigation failed to resolve this. It was stonewalled, no evidence was heard, and it was treated as "politics" and not a crucial legal issue. The talking points were about elections, forgeries, racism (Obama was the "Black Jesus"), where he was born, and other diverse issues.

He was a "Natural Born Citizen" to an American mother, born not in Kenya, but in Hawaii.

None of which mattered. All that was a diversion. Those in power wanted to keep Obama. Here is what did matter. The US Constitution.

**Article II, Section 1, Clause 5:**

*"No Person except a **natural born Citizen**, or a Citizen of the United States, at the time of the Adoption of this Constitution, shall be eligible to the Office of President; neither shall any Person be eligible to that Office who shall not have attained to the Age of thirty-five Years, and been fourteen Years a Resident within the United States."*

The deciding issue should have been the three words "**natural born Citizen**." This was somehow ignored. What is a natural born Citizen? It was not about cesarean sections. They did not exist in 1776. Nor did it say anything about the geographic location, the place of birth.

The case law, evaluated only a few times over the centuries, is quite clear about its meaning. Such a person had to have **BOTH** parents as American citizens to be "natural born."

**Does that little detail disqualify Barack Hussein Obama II as President?** It does if the person listed on the first infamous (and, yes, possibly forged) birth certificate, also named **Barack Hussein Obama**, is correct. Why? Because the father listed was **not**, and never had been, a US Citizen.

If that were the situation, Obama was **not** a legitimate President, the election would be invalid, and, thus, all the decisions he made and policies he set during his term are invalid. A situation that would cause boundless joy for some and horror for others.

Confusing the issue is that his mother later remarried, and Barack Hussein Obama II took on the name Barry Soetoro. Barry Soetoro is also **Barack Hussein Obama II.** The same person, but that is irrelevant. His birth father, as claimed, is **Barack Hussein Obama.** Who was **not** a US citizen.

Those who accepted Obama as President did so because "There is no doubt that Barack Obama is, indeed, born in the United States of America." I'm not sure we know where he was born, but under the Constitution, that doesn't matter as far as eligibility for the office is concerned.

Wow! **If that is not an issue for a bit of righteous Mind War, it is hard to imagine what might be**. As a closing comment, we suggest it may be time for a change.

Why are we allowing people to hold offices in our Federal Government (Congress, the Senate, or the Federal Bureaucracies) if they are foreign citizens or dual citizens or taking money directly or indirectly from a foreign government or firm?

Their **only** loyalty should be to the United States.

## A Reader Comment about our book

*"It is most certainly a **Mind War**. But it goes beyond the mind, all the way through the soul.*

*The same arrogance that Lucifer held, the corrupted self-image that led him to defy GOD, is manifest in his elitist followers. And, as with Satan himself, they will not relinquish this "self" orientation until their end. Satan is the religion of self. It is this religion that he has used to stir the minds of men toward self-satisfaction and the rejection of Christ.*

*But quite unlike those elites, I do not incline to attempt godhood. I'll leave that to The Professional."*

# THE AUTHORS

**Paul info:** https://www.standupamericaus.org/ e-mail: suaus1961@gmail.com

**John info:** https://www.johntrudel.com

18932681R00040